ECHO POP UNLOCKED

WITH

ALEXA FEATURES

The Complete User Guide For Beginners And Seniors

(*Tips and Tricks*)

Richard Allard

All rights reserved. No part of this publication may be reproduced, distributed, or transmitted in any form or by any means, including photocopying, recording, or other electronic or mechanical methods, without the prior written permission of the publisher, except in the case of brief quotations embodied in critical reviews and containing other non-commercial uses permitted by copyright law.

Copyright © Richard Allard, 2024.

TABLE OF CONTENT

INTRODUCTION... 3
GETTING STARTED WITH YOUR ECHO POP.............. 6
    1.1 Unboxing And Setup.. 6
    1.2 Connecting To Wi-Fi And Your Account........ 9
    Tips For A Smooth Setup Experience............... 13
MASTERING THE BASICS.. 14
    2.1 Voice Commands And Interactions............. 14
    2.2 Using The Buttons And Controls.................. 22
MUSIC AND ENTERTAINMENT................................... 29
    3.1 Streaming Music Services........................... 29
    Tips For An Enhanced Music Experience........ 37
    3.2 Podcasts And Audiobooks...................... 38
    Tips For Podcasts And Audiobooks.................. 42
SMART HOME INTEGRATION...................................... 44
    4.1 Connecting Smart Devices........................ 44
    4.2 Creating Routines And Scenes.................... 53
COMMUNICATION AND CALLING............................... 59
    5.1 Making Calls And Sending Messages......... 59
    5.2 Using Drop-In And Announcements........... 68
TROUBLESHOOTING AND TIPS................................. 74
    6.1 Common Problems And Solutions............... 74
    6.2 Maximizing Echo Pop Performance............. 84
CONCLUSION... 89
    TIPS AND TRICKS.. 92

INTRODUCTION

Welcome to the world of the **Amazon Echo Pop,** your personal voice-controlled assistant that can make your home smarter, your routines easier, and your life more enjoyable. Imagine having a helpful companion ready to play your favorite songs, control your smart lights, give you the weather forecast, make calls, or even tell you a joke, all with just a simple voice command. The Echo Pop is more than just a gadget; it's a gateway to a new level of convenience and connectivity.

In this guidebook, we'll take you step-by-step through everything you need to know about using your Echo Pop. Whether you're completely new to smart devices or have some experience with Alexa; this book will help you unlock the full potential of your Echo Pop. From setting it up for the first time to exploring its amazing features like playing music, managing smart home devices, making calls, and troubleshooting common issues, we've got you covered.

What makes the Echo Pop so special is how effortlessly it fits into your daily life. It listens, it learns, and it helps you stay connected and entertained without ever lifting a finger. In a world where time is precious, the Echo Pop simplifies tasks so you can focus on what truly matters.

Our goal with this guide is to make your experience smooth, fun, and frustration-free. We'll break down the features in easy-to-understand language, provide practical tips, and offers troubleshooting solutions that actually work. By the end of this book, you'll not only be confident using your Echo Pop, but you might also wonder how you ever lived without it.

So, let's dive in and discover how the **Amazon Echo Pop** can transform your everyday life. Your smart home adventure starts now!

CHAPTER 1

GETTING STARTED WITH YOUR ECHO POP

1.1 Unboxing And Setup

Congratulations on purchasing your Amazon Echo Pop! This guide will walk you through the process of unboxing, setting up, and preparing your device for use. With a few simple steps, you'll be ready to explore all the features of this compact and versatile smart speaker.

What's Inside the Box?

When you open the packaging, you'll find the following items:

1. **Amazon Echo Pop**: The star of the show, shaped like a half-sphere with a sleek, flat front.
2. **Power Adapter**: A cable to connect your Echo Pop to an electrical outlet.
3. **Quick Start Guide**: A small booklet that outlines the basic setup process.

Carefully remove these items from the box. Be sure to check for any protective plastic coverings on the device and cable before proceeding.

Preparing Your Space

Choose a location for your Echo Pop that meets the following criteria:

- **Flat Surface**: Place the device on a stable, flat surface like a table, countertop, or desk.

- **Proximity to Power**: Ensure the Echo Pop is near a power outlet so you can connect it easily.
- **Open Space**: For optimal sound quality, place it in an open area away from walls or obstructions.
- **Wi-Fi Signal**: Ensure the location has a strong and stable Wi-Fi signal, as this is essential for the device to work.

Powering Up Your Echo Pop

1. Plug the power adapter into the back of your Echo Pop.
2. Connect the other end of the adapter to a power outlet.
3. Wait for the light ring on the Echo Pop to illuminate. It will cycle through a

few colors before settling on orange, indicating it's ready for setup.

At this point, your Echo Pop is physically ready to connect to your home network and Alexa app.

1.2 Connecting To Wi-Fi And Your Account

Now that your Echo Pop is powered on, the next step is to connect it to your Wi-Fi network and link it to your Amazon account. This process is crucial because it allows Alexa, the virtual assistant, to perform tasks and access online features.

Step 1: Download the Alexa App

1. **Find the App**: On your smartphone or tablet, go to the **App Store** (iOS) or **Google Play Store** (Android).

2. **Search for Alexa**: Type "Amazon Alexa" in the search bar.
3. **Download and Install**: Tap the download button to install the app.

Once installed, open the app and sign in with your Amazon account. If you don't have an account, you can create one for free during the app setup.

Step 2: Begin the Setup Process

1. **Launch the Alexa App**: Open the app and select "Devices" from the bottom menu.
2. **Add a Device**: Tap the "+" icon in the top-right corner, then choose "Add Device."

3. **Select Device Type**: From the list of device options, select "Amazon Echo" and then choose "Echo Pop."

Step 3: Connect to Wi-Fi

1. **Wait for the Orange Light**: Ensure the light ring on your Echo Pop is orange. This indicates the device is in setup mode.
2. **Choose Your Echo Pop**: In the app, you should see "Echo Pop" appear as a device ready to connect. Tap on it.
3. **Select Your Wi-Fi Network**: The app will prompt you to choose your Wi-Fi network. Select it and enter your password.

Once connected, the light ring on your Echo Pop will turn blue, indicating that it's online and ready to use.

Step 4: Link Your Amazon Account

During the setup, the app will ask you to confirm or log in with your Amazon account. This step ensures that all your preferences, shopping lists, and Alexa Skills are linked to your Echo Pop.

Step 5: Test Your Echo Pop

To confirm that everything is working, try saying, **"Alexa, what's the weather?"** If Alexa responds with the current weather, congratulations! Your Echo Pop is set up and ready to use.

Tips For A Smooth Setup Experience

- **Check Wi-Fi Strength**: If your device has trouble connecting, move it closer to your router during setup.
- **Update the App**: Ensure the Alexa app is updated to the latest version for the best experience.
- **Reboot If Needed**: If the orange light doesn't appear, unplug the Echo Pop for a minute and plug it back in.

Chapter 2

MASTERING THE BASICS

2.1 Voice Commands And Interactions

The Echo Pop is designed to make your life easier by allowing you to use your voice to interact with Alexa, the smart assistant. Learning the basics of voice commands and interactions will help you unlock the full potential of your Echo Pop. In this section, we'll explore how to speak to Alexa, understand basic and advanced commands, and get Alexa to respond to you accurately.

How to Wake Alexa

To interact with your Echo Pop, you need to **wake Alexa** by using a **wake word**. The default wake word is **"Alexa"**. Whenever you say this word, the light ring on your Echo Pop will turn blue, signaling that Alexa is listening and ready to take your command.

If you want to change the wake word, you can do so through the **Alexa app**:

1. Open the Alexa app on your smartphone or tablet.
2. Go to **Devices**.
3. Select your **Echo Pop** from the list.
4. Tap on **Settings** and look for the **Wake Word** option.

5. Choose from alternative wake words like **"Echo," "Amazon,"** or **"Computer."**

Basic Voice Commands

Now that you know how to wake Alexa, let's try some basic commands. These simple requests help you get familiar with interacting with your Echo Pop.

1. **Asking the Time and Date**:

    - *"Alexa, what time is it?"*
    - *"Alexa, what's the date today?"*

2. **Getting Weather Updates**:

    - *"Alexa, what's the weather like today?"*
    - *"Alexa, will it rain tomorrow?"*

3. **Setting Alarms and Timers**:

    - *"Alexa, set an alarm for 7 a.m."*
    - *"Alexa, set a timer for 20 minutes."*

4. **Playing Music**:

    - *"Alexa, play some relaxing music."*
    - *"Alexa, play 'Imagine' by John Lennon."*

5. **General Information**:

    - *"Alexa, who is the President of the United States?"*
    - *"Alexa, how far is the Moon?"*

6. **Controlling Smart Home Devices** (if connected):

- "Alexa, turn off the living room lights."
- "Alexa, set the thermostat to 72 degrees."

Advanced Voice Commands

As you become more comfortable with basic commands, you can start using more advanced commands that involve multiple steps or more personalized interactions. Here are some examples:

1. **Creating a Shopping List**:

    - "Alexa, add milk, bread, and eggs to my shopping list."
    - To check your list, say, "Alexa, what's on my shopping list?"

2. **Checking News Updates**:

    - *"Alexa, what's my flash briefing?"*
    This will give you a short summary of the latest news from your selected sources.

3. **Setting Routines**:

    - Routines are sets of motions set off by one command.
    For example: *"Alexa, good morning."*
    This can turn on the lights, give you the weather, and play the news.

4. **Asking for a Joke**:

- *"Alexa, tell me a joke."*

  Alexa has a library of fun and quirky jokes to entertain you.

5. **Translations**:

   - *"Alexa, how do you say 'good morning' in Spanish?"*

Improving Alexa's Understanding

Sometimes Alexa might not understand your command correctly. Here are a few tips to improve communication:

1. **Speak Clearly**: Use a calm and clear voice.
2. **Be Specific**: The more precise your command, the better Alexa understands.

For example, instead of *"Play music,"* say *"Play pop music from the 1990s."*

3. **Rephrase If Needed**: If Alexa doesn't get it right, try saying the same thing in a different way.
4. **Check Alexa App Feedback**: The Alexa app shows a history of your interactions and lets you see what Alexa heard. This can help you understand why a command didn't work.

Ending Interactions

To stop Alexa from performing a task, you can use phrases like:

- *"Alexa, stop."*
- *"Alexa, cancel."*

If you're listening to music or a timer is ringing, these commands will pause or stop the activity immediately.

2.2 Using The Buttons And Controls

While voice commands are the primary way to interact with your Echo Pop, it also has a few **physical buttons and controls** that can come in handy. These buttons allow you to quickly perform tasks or make adjustments without using your voice. Let's go over each button, what it does, and when you might want to use it.

Overview of Buttons on the Echo Pop

On the top of the Echo Pop, you'll find the following buttons:

1. **Action Button (•)**:

    - This button has a small dot symbol on it.
    - **Function**: Pressing the Action button wakes Alexa without using the wake word. It can also be used to reset the device or set it up manually.
    - **When to Use**:
        - If you're in a noisy environment where Alexa might not hear you clearly.
        - When you want to quickly activate Alexa without speaking.
2. **Volume Up (+) Button**:

- **Function**: Increases the volume of the Echo Pop.
- **When to Use**:
  - If you want to make Alexa's responses or music louder.
- **Tip**: You can also adjust the volume with your voice by saying, *"Alexa, increase the volume."*

3. **Volume Down (−) Button**:

   - **Function**: Decreases the volume of the Echo Pop.
   - **When to Use**:
     - If Alexa is too loud or you want to lower the music volume.

- **Tip**: You can say, *"Alexa, lower the volume."*

4. **Microphone Off Button** (with a microphone symbol and a slash):

  - **Function**: Turns off the microphone, so Alexa stops listening for wake words. When this button is pressed, the light ring turns **red** to indicate that the microphone is disabled.
  - **When to Use**:
    - If you want privacy and don't want Alexa to respond to wake words.
  - **Tip**: To re-enable the microphone, press the button again. The light ring will turn

off, indicating that Alexa is listening again.

Understanding the Light Ring

The Echo Pop's **light ring** is a key part of understanding your device's status. Here's a quick guide to the different light colors and what they mean:

1. **Blue Light**:

    o Alexa is listening or processing your request.

2. **Orange Light**:

    o The device is in setup mode or trying to connect to Wi-Fi.

3. **Red Light**:

- The microphone is off.

4. **Yellow Light**:

    - You have a message or notification.
    - To check messages, say, *"Alexa, what are my notifications?"*

5. **Green Light**:

    - You have an incoming call or drop-in.

Combining Buttons and Voice Commands

Sometimes, using a combination of buttons and voice commands can be the most efficient way to interact with your Echo Pop. For example:

- **Pause Music**: You can say, *"Alexa, stop,"* or press the **Action button** to stop playback.
- **Adjust Volume**: Use the **Volume buttons** for quick adjustments, or say, *"Alexa, set the volume to 5."*

CHAPTER 3

MUSIC AND ENTERTAINMENT

3.1 Streaming Music Services

One of the most popular uses of the Echo Pop is enjoying music and other audio entertainment. Whether you want to listen to your favorite artists, discover new songs, or simply relax to background music, the Echo Pop makes it easy and fun. In this section, we'll cover everything you need to know about using streaming music services with your Echo Pop, including how to set them up, give voice commands, and customize your listening experience.

What Are Streaming Music Services?

Streaming music services allow you to listen to millions of songs over the internet without needing to download them. Some of the most common services compatible with the Echo Pop include:

1. **Amazon Music** (Free, Prime, and Unlimited)
2. **Spotify** (Free and Premium)
3. **Apple Music**
4. **Pandora**
5. **SiriusXM**
6. **Tidal**
7. **iHeartRadio**

Each of these services has its own library of songs, playlists, and features. Some services are free but come with ads, while others require a paid subscription for an ad-free experience and extra features.

Setting Up a Streaming Music Service

To enjoy music on your Echo Pop, you first need to link your preferred streaming service through the **Alexa app**. Here's a step-by-step guide to setting up a music service:

1. **Open the Alexa App**: Launch the app on your smartphone or tablet.
2. **Go to Settings**: Tap on **More** (the three horizontal lines) and select **Settings**.
3. **Select Music & Podcasts**: This option will show you the list of available music services.

4. **Link a New Service**: Tap **Link New Service** and choose the service you want (e.g., Spotify, Apple Music, Amazon Music).
5. **Sign In**: Follow the prompts to sign in with your service account. You may need to enter your username and password.
6. **Set as Default** (Optional): If you want this to be your primary music service, tap **Set as Default Music Service**.

Now that your music service is linked, you're ready to play your favorite songs with a simple voice command!

Playing Music with Voice Commands

Once your preferred music service is set up, you can ask Alexa to play songs, artists, genres, and more. Here are some common voice commands you can use:

1. **Play a Specific Song**:

    - *"Alexa, play 'Shape of You' by Ed Sheeran."*

2. **Play an Artist**:

    - *"Alexa, play songs by Taylor Swift."*

3. **Play a Genre**:

    - *"Alexa, play classical music."*
    - *"Alexa, play some jazz."*

4. **Play a Playlist**:

    - *"Alexa, play my workout playlist."*
    - *"Alexa, play the Top 50 hits."*

5. **Play an Album**:

    - *"Alexa, play the album 'Thriller' by Michael Jackson."*

6. **Control Playback**:

    - *"Alexa, pause."*
    - *"Alexa, resume."*
    - *"Alexa, skip this song."*
    - *"Alexa, play the previous song."*

7. **Adjust Volume**:

    - *"Alexa, turn up the volume."*

- *"Alexa, set the volume to 5."* (Volume levels range from 0 to 10.)

Exploring Amazon Music Options

If you're an Amazon customer, you have access to different tiers of **Amazon Music**:

1. **Amazon Music Free**: Offers a limited selection of songs with ads.
2. **Amazon Prime Music**: Included with your Amazon Prime membership, giving you access to over 2 million songs without ads.
3. **Amazon Music Unlimited**: A subscription service that gives you access to over 90 million songs, playlists, and podcasts, all ad-free.

You can upgrade to **Amazon Music Unlimited** through the Alexa app or by saying:

- *"Alexa, upgrade to Amazon Music Unlimited."*

Using Spotify with Alexa

If you're a **Spotify** user, you can link your account to Alexa and enjoy your playlists, albums, and recommendations. After linking Spotify to the Alexa app, you can say:

- *"Alexa, play my Discover Weekly playlist on Spotify."*
- *"Alexa, play 'Blinding Lights' on Spotify."*

If you have a **Spotify Premium** account, you can enjoy an ad-free experience and higher-quality audio.

Tips For An Enhanced Music Experience

1. **Create Custom Playlists**: Build playlists in your streaming service app and ask Alexa to play them.
2. **Set a Music Alarm**: Wake up to your favorite song by saying, *"Alexa, set an alarm for 7 a.m. to 'Happy' by Pharrell Williams."*
3. **Loop Songs**: To repeat a song, say, *"Alexa, loop this song."*
4. **Discover New Music**: Ask Alexa to play popular hits or trending songs: *"Alexa, play the latest pop hits."*

3.2 Podcasts And Audiobooks

In addition to music, your Echo Pop is a great device for listening to **podcasts** and **audiobooks**. These audio formats are perfect for learning something new, enjoying stories, or keeping yourself entertained during chores or relaxation time.

What Are Podcasts?

Podcasts are audio programs similar to radio shows, but you can listen to them anytime you want. They cover a wide range of topics, including news, education, true crime, comedy, and more.

Some popular podcast platforms that work with Alexa include:

1. **Amazon Music** (supports podcasts)

2. **Apple Podcasts**
3. **Spotify**
4. **TuneIn**
5. **iHeartRadio**

How to Play Podcasts on Echo Pop

To play a podcast, make sure your preferred podcast service is linked in the Alexa app. Then use simple voice commands like:

1. **Play a Specific Podcast**:

    - "Alexa, play 'The Daily' podcast."
    - "Alexa, play 'Stuff You Should Know' podcast."

2. **Play the Latest Episode**:

- "*Alexa, play the latest episode of 'Crime Junkie.'*"

3. **Control Podcast Playback**:

    - "*Alexa, pause the podcast.*"
    - "*Alexa, resume the podcast.*"
    - "*Alexa, skip forward 30 seconds.*"
    - "*Alexa, go back 10 seconds.*"

What Are Audiobooks?

Audiobooks are recorded versions of books read aloud. They are perfect for when you want to enjoy a book but don't have the time to sit down and read. Audiobooks are available through services like:

1. **Audible**: The most popular audiobook service, owned by Amazon.

2. **Amazon Kindle**: Some Kindle books come with free audio narration.

How to Play Audiobooks on Echo Pop

To listen to an audiobook, link your Audible account or Kindle account through the Alexa app. Once linked, you can use commands like:

1. **Start an Audiobook**:

    - *"Alexa, play my audiobook 'Harry Potter and the Sorcerer's Stone.'"*

2. **Control Playback**:

    - *"Alexa, pause the book."*
    - *"Alexa, resume the book."*
    - *"Alexa, go to chapter 3."*

3. **Check Your Library**:

    ○ *"Alexa, what audiobooks do I have?"*

4. **Set a Sleep Timer**:

    ○ *"Alexa, stop reading in 30 minutes."*
    This is great for bedtime listening!

Tips For Podcasts And Audiobooks

1. **Find New Content**:

    ○ *"Alexa, recommend a podcast."*
    ○ *"Alexa, suggest an audiobook."*

2. **Multitask**: Listen to podcasts or audiobooks while cooking, cleaning, or

exercising.

3. **Sync Progress**: If you listen on another device, Alexa will pick up where you left off.

CHAPTER 4

SMART HOME INTEGRATION

4.1 Connecting Smart Devices

One of the most exciting features of the **Echo Pop** is its ability to connect to and control smart home devices. Imagine turning on the lights, adjusting the thermostat, or locking the doors, all with a simple voice command. Alexa makes managing your smart home convenient and fun, even for beginners.

In this section, we'll walk you through what smart home devices are, how to connect them to your Echo Pop, and how to start controlling them with Alexa.

What Are Smart Home Devices?

Smart home devices are everyday household items that can connect to the internet and be controlled remotely, usually through an app or a voice assistant like Alexa. These devices can include:

1. **Smart Lights**: Bulbs, lamps, or switches you can turn on or off and dim using your voice.
2. **Smart Plugs**: Outlets that let you control plugged-in devices like coffee makers or fans.
3. **Smart Thermostats**: Devices that control your home's temperature,

allowing you to adjust heating or cooling with voice commands.

4. **Smart Cameras and Doorbells**: Security cameras and video doorbells you can monitor through your phone or Echo device.
5. **Smart Locks**: Locks that can be locked or unlocked remotely.
6. **Smart TVs and Speakers**: Entertainment systems you can turn on, off, or control using Alexa.
7. **Smart Sensors**: Motion, temperature, and contact sensors are used to monitor your home.

Most smart home devices connect via **Wi-Fi**, but some may use other wireless technologies like **Bluetooth** or **Zigbee**. The Echo Pop can work with many types of devices, making it easy to build a smart home setup.

Choosing Compatible Smart Devices

Before connecting smart devices to your Echo Pop, it's important to ensure they are **compatible with Alexa**. Most modern smart devices will clearly state on the packaging or in the product description if they work with Alexa. Look for labels like:

- "Works with Alexa"
- "Alexa Compatible"

Popular smart home brands that work seamlessly with Alexa include:

- **Philips Hue** (smart lighting)
- **TP-Link Kasa** (smart plugs and switches)

- **Ring** (video doorbells and cameras)
- **Nest** (thermostats and cameras)
- **August** (smart locks)
- **Ecobee** (smart thermostats)

Setting Up Smart Devices with the Alexa App

Connecting smart home devices to your Echo Pop involves linking them through the **Alexa app**. Here's a step-by-step guide to help you get started:

1. **Install the Device**:

    Follow the manufacturer's instructions to install the smart device. This usually involves plugging it in, setting it up through its own app, and connecting it to your Wi-Fi network.

2. **Open the Alexa App**:

    Launch the Alexa app on your smartphone or tablet.

3. **Go to Devices**:

    Tap on the **Devices** tab at the bottom of the screen.

4. **Add Device**:

    Tap the + **(Plus)** button in the top-right corner and select **Add Device**.

5. **Select Device Type**:

    Choose the type of device you're adding, such as **Light**, **Plug**, **Thermostat**, or **Camera**.

6. **Select Brand**:

   Pick the brand of your smart device (e.g., **Philips Hue**, **TP-Link**, or **Nest**).

7. **Follow the Prompts**:

   The app will guide you through the process of linking the device. You may need to sign in to your device's account to complete the connection.

8. **Discover Devices**:

   Once linked, Alexa will automatically discover your device. You can also say:

   - *"Alexa, discover my devices."*

9. **Name Your Device**:

   Give your device a simple name like **"Living Room Light"** or **"Kitchen**

Plug" so Alexa can easily understand your commands.

Controlling Your Smart Devices

Now that your smart devices are connected, you can control them with voice commands. Here are some examples:

1. **Lights**:

    - *"Alexa, turn on the living room lights."*
    - *"Alexa, dim the bedroom lights to 50%."*
    - *"Alexa, turn off the kitchen lights."*

2. **Plugs**:

- "Alexa, turn on the coffee maker."
- "Alexa, turn off the fan."

3. **Thermostats**:

    - "Alexa, set the thermostat to 72 degrees."
    - "Alexa, increase the temperature by 2 degrees."

4. **Locks**:

    - "Alexa, lock the front door."
    - "Alexa, is the back door locked?"

5. **Cameras and Doorbells**:

    - "Alexa, show me the front door camera."
    - "Alexa, answer the door."

You can also check the status of your devices by asking Alexa:

- *"Alexa, is the living room light on?"*
- *"Alexa, what's the temperature in the house?"*

4.2 Creating Routines And Scenes

Once you're comfortable controlling individual smart devices, you can make your smart home even more convenient by setting up **Routines** and **Scenes**. These features let you automate multiple tasks with a single voice command or a scheduled trigger.

What Are Routines?

Routines are a way to automate a series of actions based on a trigger. For example, you can create a routine to turn on the lights and start playing music when you say, *"Alexa, good morning."*

Setting Up a Routine

Follow these steps to create a routine in the Alexa app:

1. **Open the Alexa App**: Launch the app on your device.

2. **Go to Routines**: Tap **More** (the three horizontal lines) and select **Routines**.

3. **Create a New Routine**: Tap the + **(Plus)** button to start a new routine.

4. **Add a Trigger**: Choose what will trigger the routine. This could be:

    - **Voice Command**: Something you say, like *"Alexa, bedtime."*
    - **Schedule**: A specific time, like every morning at 7 a.m.
    - **Device Action**: When a motion sensor detects movement or a door is opened.
5. **Add Actions**: Choose what Alexa should do when the routine is triggered. Examples include:

    - Turning on or off lights.
    - Playing a playlist.
    - Giving you the weather report.

6. **Save the Routine**: Tap **Save** to activate your routine.

Now, whenever you use the trigger, Alexa will perform the actions you've set up.

Examples of Useful Routines

1. **Morning Routine**:

    o Trigger: *"Alexa, good morning."*
    o Actions: Turn on the bedroom lights, read the weather, and play the news.
2. **Bedtime Routine**:

    o Trigger: *"Alexa, bedtime."*

- Actions: Turn off all lights, lock the doors, and play relaxing music.

3. **Leaving Home Routine**:

    - Trigger: *"Alexa, I'm leaving."*
    - Actions: Turn off lights, lower the thermostat, and activate security cameras.

What Are Scenes?

Scenes are similar to routines but focus mainly on smart home devices. They allow you to set multiple devices to a specific state with a single command. For example:

- **Movie Night Scene**: Turn on the TV, darken the lights, and close the blinds.

You can set up scenes using smart device apps like **Philips Hue** or **Kasa**, then link those scenes to Alexa for voice control.

Creating a Scene with Alexa

1. **Set Up Scenes in Device App**: Use your smart device app to create a scene (e.g., "Movie Night").
2. **Discover Scenes with Alexa**: Say, *"Alexa, discover my scenes."*
3. **Activate Scene**: Say, *"Alexa, turn on Movie Night."*

CHAPTER 5

COMMUNICATION AND CALLING

5.1 Making Calls And Sending Messages

One of the most valuable features of your **Amazon Echo Pop** is its ability to help you stay in touch with family and friends. You can make hands-free voice calls, send messages, and even connect with people who also have Alexa-enabled devices. This makes communication quick, easy, and fun, especially when you're busy with household tasks or want to chat without picking up your phone.

In this section, we'll explore how to set up calls, make calls, and send messages using your Echo Pop and Alexa.

Setting Up Communication Features

Before you can start making calls and sending messages with Alexa, you need to set up the communication features in the **Alexa app**. Here's a step-by-step guide to get you started:

1. **Open the Alexa App**:

    Launch the Alexa app on your smartphone or tablet.

2. **Go to the Communicate Tab**:

    Tap the **Communicate** icon at the

bottom of the screen. It looks like a speech bubble.

3. **Grant Permissions**:

   The app will ask for permission to access your contacts and phone number. Grant these permissions so Alexa can sync with your contacts.

4. **Verify Your Phone Number**:

   Enter your phone number and verify it using the code sent via SMS. This allows Alexa to identify your phone number and connect you with your contacts.

5. **Sync Contacts**:

   Alexa will ask to sync your contacts. This allows you to call and message people in your phone's contact list who also use Alexa.

6. **Enable Calling and Messaging**:

Follow the prompts to enable calling and messaging. Once everything is set up, you're ready to start communicating.

Making Calls with Alexa

Once you've set up communication features, making calls with your Echo Pop is simple. You can call other Alexa-enabled devices or even regular phone numbers in certain countries. Here's how you can make calls:

1. **To Call a Contact**:

If the person you want to call is in

your contacts and has an Alexa device, say:

- *"Alexa, call [John]."*

   Alexa will call John's Alexa device or mobile phone, depending on his settings.

2. **To Call a Phone Number**:

   You can call a specific phone number directly. Just say:

   - *"Alexa, call 555-123-4567."*

3. **Answering Calls**:

   When you receive a call on your Echo Pop, Alexa will announce the caller's name. To answer, say:

   - *"Alexa, answer the call."*

4. **Ending Calls**:

   When you're ready to hang up, simply say:

   ○ *"Alexa, hang up."*

5. **Making Emergency Calls**:

   Alexa does **not** support emergency services (like 911). Always use your phone for emergency calls.

Tips for Making Calls

- **Check Your Wi-Fi**:

   Ensure your Echo Pop is connected to Wi-Fi; calls won't work without an internet connection.

- **Clear Pronunciation**:

   Speak clearly when saying the name

of the person you want to call. This helps Alexa recognize the contact.

- **Privacy Considerations**:

    Anyone nearby can hear your conversation, so be aware when making private calls.

Sending Messages with Alexa

In addition to calls, your Echo Pop can also send voice and text messages. This is great for quick reminders or messages when your hands are busy. Here's how to send messages with Alexa:

1. **Sending a Voice Message**:

    You can send a voice recording to your contacts. Just say:

- *"Alexa, send a message to [Mom]."*

  Alexa will ask you to record your message. Once you're done, say: *"Send it."*

2. **Sending a Text Message**:

   If you prefer to send a text message, Alexa can convert your voice to text. Say:

   - *"Alexa, send a message to [Sarah]: I'll be there in 10 minutes."*

3. **Listening to Messages**:

   When someone sends you a message, Alexa will notify you by saying:

   - *"You have a message from [Dad]."*

To hear it, say: *"Alexa, play my messages."*

4. **Checking Messages**:

   To check if you have any unread messages, say:

   - *"Alexa, do I have any messages?"*

5. **Deleting Messages**:

   You can delete old messages by saying:

   - *"Alexa, delete all my messages."*

Tips for Sending Messages

- **Speak Clearly**:

  Speak slowly and clearly when dictating messages to avoid mistakes.

- **Notification Settings**:

    Make sure your Alexa app notifications are enabled so you get alerts for new messages.

- **Voice and Text Options**:

    Alexa gives you the option to send either voice recordings or text messages, depending on your preference.

5.2 Using Drop-In And Announcements

In addition to calling and messaging, Alexa offers two unique communication features: **Drop-In** and **Announcements**. These features make it easy to communicate within your household or instantly connect with loved ones.

Using Drop-In

Drop-In is like having an intercom system in your home. It lets you connect instantly to another Alexa device without waiting for the person to answer. This is useful for quick check-ins, like letting family members know dinner is ready or asking someone a question in another room.

How to Enable Drop-In

To use Drop-In, you need to enable it in the Alexa app. Here's how:

1. **Open the Alexa App**: Launch the app on your phone or tablet.

2. **Go to Devices**: Tap the **Devices** icon at the bottom.

3. **Select Your Echo Pop**: Choose the device you want to enable Drop-In for.

4. **Enable Drop-In**: Tap **Communications** and then **Drop-In**. Select **On** to enable it.

You can also grant Drop-In permissions to specific contacts, like close family members.

How to Use Drop-In

Once Drop-In is enabled, you can connect to other Alexa devices in your home or with approved contacts. Here's how:

1. **Drop-In on a Specific Device:**

   Say: *"Alexa, Drop-In on [Living Room Echo]."* You'll immediately be connected to that device.

2. **Drop-In on Approved Contacts:**

   If a family member has approved Drop-In, you can say:

   o *"Alexa, Drop-In on [Mom]."*

3. **Ending Drop-In:**

   To end a Drop-In session, say:

   o *"Alexa, hang up."*

When to Use Drop-In

- **Checking on Family:** Quickly check in on kids or elderly family members.

- **Household Announcements**: Let people know dinner is ready or that it's time to leave.
- **Instant Communication**: Use Drop-In for instant communication without needing a phone call.

Using Announcements

Announcements are one-way messages that Alexa broadcasts to all your Alexa-enabled devices. Think of it as making a public announcement to your household. This is useful for sharing quick messages like:

- **"Dinner is ready!"**
- **"Time to get up!"**

How to Make an Announcement

To make an announcement, say:

- *"Alexa, announce that dinner is ready."*

Alexa will repeat your message on all your Echo devices with a chime.

Examples of Announcements

1. **Morning Routine**:

   - *"Alexa, announce that it's time to wake up."*

2. **Leaving the House**:

   - *"Alexa, announce that we're leaving in 5 minutes."*

3. **Reminders**:

   - *"Alexa, announce that homework time is starting."*

CHAPTER 6

TROUBLESHOOTING AND TIPS

6.1 Common Problems And Solutions

Even though the **Amazon Echo Pop** is a reliable and user-friendly device, like any technology, you may occasionally run into issues. The good news is that most of these problems have simple solutions. In this section, we'll cover some of the most common issues you might face and how to resolve them step by step. Whether your Echo Pop isn't responding or there are connectivity issues, you'll find helpful solutions here.

1. Alexa Isn't Responding

Problem:

You give Alexa a command, but she doesn't respond, or she says, "I'm having trouble understanding right now."

Solution:

1. **Check the Microphone:**

    Make sure the microphone isn't turned off. If the microphone button on the top of your Echo Pop is red, press it to turn the microphone back on.

2. **Check the Wi-Fi Connection:**

    If Alexa says she can't understand or is unresponsive, it might be due to a poor internet connection. To fix this:

- Say: *"Alexa, are you connected to the internet?"*
- If she says no, try reconnecting to Wi-Fi using the Alexa app:
    1. Open the Alexa app.
    2. Go to **Devices** > **Echo & Alexa** > select your Echo Pop.
    3. Tap **Change** next to Wi-Fi and follow the prompts to reconnect.

3. **Restart Your Echo Pop**:

Sometimes, a simple restart can fix the problem. Unplug your Echo Pop, wait 30 seconds, and plug it back in.

2. Echo Pop Can't Connect to Wi-Fi

Problem:

Your Echo Pop keeps disconnecting from the internet or won't connect to Wi-Fi during setup.

Solution:

1. **Check Your Router:**

    Ensure your router is turned on and working properly. Try restarting it by unplugging it for 30 seconds and plugging it back in.

2. **Check Wi-Fi Signal Strength:**

    Your Echo Pop might be too far from the router. Move it closer and see if that improves connectivity.

3. **Reconnect to Wi-Fi**:

   To reconnect manually:

   1. Open the Alexa app.
   2. Go to **Devices** > **Echo & Alexa** > select your Echo Pop.
   3. Tap **Change Wi-Fi** and follow the instructions.

4. **Check for Interference**:

   Check that the transmission is not being interfered with by any electronic equipment or objects. Microwaves, baby monitors, and cordless phones can disrupt Wi-Fi.

3. Alexa Doesn't Understand Your Commands

Problem:

Alexa misinterprets your requests or says she doesn't understand what you're asking.

Solution:

1. **Speak Clearly:**

    Make sure you are speaking clearly and at a normal volume.

2. **Use Simple Commands:**

    Try breaking your commands into simpler phrases. Instead of saying, *"Alexa, can you play my upbeat workout playlist on Spotify?"* Try *"Alexa, play workout music on Spotify."*

3. **Check for Updates**:

    Ensure your Echo Pop has the latest software update. Alexa updates automatically when connected to Wi-Fi, but you can check by saying:

    - *"Alexa, check for updates."*

4. **Rephrase Your Request**:

    Sometimes, rephrasing your question can help Alexa understand better.

4. Music or Audio Isn't Playing

Problem:

When you ask Alexa to play music or a podcast, nothing happens, or the audio cuts out.

Solution:

1. **Check Your Subscription**:

    If you're using a streaming service like **Spotify**, **Amazon Music**, or **Apple Music**, ensure your subscription is active.

2. **Check the Volume**:

    Sometimes the volume might be too low. Say:

    - *"Alexa, volume up."*

3. **Select the Right Device**:

    If you have multiple Alexa devices, make sure you're directing the command to the correct one.

4. **Restart Your Echo Pop**:

    Unplug it, wait 30 seconds, and plug

it back in.

5. Bluetooth Pairing Issues

Problem:

Your Echo Pop isn't connecting to a Bluetooth device.

Solution:

1. **Check Bluetooth Settings**:

    Ensure your Bluetooth device is in pairing mode.

2. **Disconnect and Reconnect**:

    - Say: *"Alexa, disconnect."*
    - Then say, "Alexa, *connect to [device name]."*

3. **Restart Both Devices**:

    Turn off Bluetooth on your device, restart your Echo Pop, and try again.

6. Echo Pop Not Responding to Routines

Problem:

Your Echo Pop isn't performing the routines you've set up.

Solution:

1. **Check Routine Settings**:

    Open the Alexa app and ensure the routine is set up correctly.

2. **Check for Triggers**:

    Make sure the routine has the right

trigger, like a specific phrase or time.

6.2 Maximizing Echo Pop Performance

Now that we've covered troubleshooting common problems, let's look at how to get the best performance out of your **Echo Pop**. These tips will help you use Alexa more effectively and make your device work smoothly.

1. Optimize Placement

Where you place your Echo Pop can impact its performance. Here are some placement tips:

1. **Central Location**:

    Place your Echo Pop in a central location in your home where it can hear you easily.

2. **Avoid Obstacles**:

Keep it away from walls, large furniture, or curtains that could block the microphone or speaker.

3. **Avoid Electronics**:

Don't place it near TVs, speakers, or microwaves, as these can interfere with its signal.

2. Use Shortcuts for Efficiency

Create **voice shortcuts** to save time. For example:

- Instead of saying, *"Alexa, turn off the living room light and the kitchen light,"* create a routine called *"Goodnight"* that does this with a single command.

3. Enable Skills

Skills are like apps for Alexa that add new features. To find and enable skills:

1. Open the Alexa app.
2. Tap **More** > **Skills & Games**.
3. Browse or search for skills like **news updates, fitness routines, or games**.

Some popular skills include **Spotify**, **Pandora**, and **Audible**.

4. Keep Your Software Updated

Alexa devices update automatically, but make sure your Echo Pop is connected to Wi-Fi to receive updates. Say:

- *"Alexa, check for updates."*

5. Use Voice Profiles

Set up **Voice Profiles** for each family member. Alexa can recognize who is speaking and provide personalized responses.

1. Open the Alexa app.
2. Go to **Settings** > **Account Settings** > **Recognized Voices**.
3. Follow the steps to create a voice profile.

6. Manage Privacy Settings

To keep your information safe, review your privacy settings:

1. Open the Alexa app.
2. Go to **Settings** > **Alexa Privacy**.
3. Adjust settings for voice recordings and data privacy.

CONCLUSION

Congratulations on reaching the end of this guidebook! By now, you should be well-equipped to make the most out of your **Amazon Echo Pop**. From setting up your device and mastering voice commands to integrating smart home gadgets, managing entertainment, making calls, and troubleshooting issues you have explored the full spectrum of what the Echo Pop can do. This little device is more than just a speaker; it's a personal assistant, a smart home hub, and a source of endless entertainment.

The beauty of the Echo Pop lies in its simplicity and power. With just a few words, you can control your environment, streamline your daily tasks, and stay connected with friends and family. As you continue to explore Alexa's capabilities, you'll discover even more ways to simplify your routines, learn new skills, and make life more enjoyable.

Remember, technology is here to serve *you*. Don't hesitate to experiment with new features, enable skills that align with your interests, and create routines that fit your lifestyle. Alexa is constantly evolving, and as updates roll out, your Echo Pop will continue to get smarter and more capable.

If you encounter challenges along the way, don't worry the troubleshooting tips in this guide are here to help. With patience and curiosity, you'll continue to unlock more potential from your device.

Thank you for choosing this guide to accompany you on your Echo Pop journey. We hope it has made your experience smooth, informative, and fun. Your smart home adventure is just beginning, and the possibilities are endless. Now, go ahead and enjoy the convenience, entertainment, and connectivity that the **Echo Pop** brings to your life.

Happy exploring, and may Alexa always be ready to assist you!

TIPS AND TRICKS

1. Customize Alexa's Wake Word

You don't have to stick with "Alexa." You can change the wake word to "Echo," "Amazon," or "Computer."

- **How to do it:** Open the **Alexa app** > **Devices** > **Echo & Alexa** > Choose your device > **Wake Word.**

2. Create Routines for Automation

Automate multiple tasks with a single voice command. For example, create a "Good Morning" routine that turns on the lights, gives the weather, and plays music.

- **How to do it:** In the Alexa app, go to **Routines > Create Routine** and set the trigger and actions.

3. Use Alexa as an Intercom

You can communicate with other Alexa devices in your home by saying, **"Alexa, Drop-In on [device name]."**

- Great for calling everyone to dinner or checking in on another room.

4. Whisper Mode for Quiet Responses

Alexa can respond in a whisper if you whisper to her, perfect for when others are asleep.

- To enable, say: **"Alexa, turn on Whisper Mode."**

5. Adjust Alexa's Voice Speed

You can make Alexa speak faster or slower to suit your preferences.

- Say: **"Alexa, speak faster"** or **"Alexa, speak slower."**

6. Set Multiple Timers and Alarms

Need to track several things at once? Alexa can handle multiple timers and alarms.

- Example: **"Alexa, set a 10-minute pasta timer"** and **"Alexa, set a 30-minute laundry timer."**

7. Use Alexa to Identify Songs

If you hear a song and don't know the title, just say, **"Alexa, what song is this?"**

- Alexa can identify the song playing through the device.

8. Play Relaxing Sounds for Sleep

Echo Pop can play ambient sounds like rain, ocean waves, or white noise.

- Example: **"Alexa, play rain sounds"** or **"Alexa, play sleep sounds."**

9. Control Smart Home Devices

Connect compatible smart devices and control them with your voice.

- Example: **"Alexa, turn off the bedroom lights"** or **"Alexa, set the thermostat to 72 degrees."**

10. Find Your Phone

Misplaced your phone? If you enable the "Find My Phone" skill, Alexa can call it for you.

- Say: **"Alexa, find my phone."**

11. Check Traffic and Commute Times

Get real-time traffic updates before you leave the house.

- Example: **"Alexa, what's the traffic like to work?"**

12. Connect Your Echo Pop to Bluetooth

Use the Echo Pop as a Bluetooth speaker for your phone.

- Say, "**Alexa, pair Bluetooth,**" and connect through your phone's Bluetooth settings.

13. Set Up Parental Controls

Enable parental controls to manage what your kids can do with Alexa.

- Use the **Amazon Parent Dashboard** for settings.

14. Enable Brief Mode

Alexa will give shorter responses to reduce chatter.

- Say: **"Alexa, turn on Brief Mode."**

15. Get Weather and News Briefings

Stay updated with quick news summaries and weather reports.

- Say: **"Alexa, what's the weather today?"** or **"Alexa, give me my Flash Briefing."**

16. Use Alexa Guard for Home Security

Alexa can help you monitor your home for unusual sounds like breaking glass or alarms when you're away.

- **How to activate:** Say, **"Alexa, I'm leaving,"** to enable Guard mode.
- Alexa will notify you if it detects something suspicious.

17. Set Up Multi-Room Music

Play music on multiple Echo devices simultaneously for a synchronized experience.

- **How to do it:** Open the **Alexa app** > **Devices** > + icon > **Combine speakers** > **Multi-room music.**

18. Schedule Reminders and To-Do Lists

Alexa can keep track of your tasks and remind you at the right time.

- Example: **"Alexa, remind me to take my medicine at 8 PM."**
- To check tasks: **"Alexa, what's on my to-do list?"**

19. Read Kindle Books Aloud

If you have Kindle books, Alexa can read them to you.

- Say, **"Alexa, read my Kindle book,"** or specify the title.

20. Enable Follow-Up Mode

Alexa can listen for additional commands without repeating the wake word.

- **How to enable:** In the Alexa app, go to **Devices** > Select your Echo Pop > **Follow-Up Mode.**

21. Customize News Sources

You can personalize your Flash Briefing by selecting your favorite news outlets.

- **How to do it:** Open the Alexa app > **Settings** > **News** > **Flash Briefing.**

22. Use Drop-In to Check on Family Members

With permission, you can "Drop-In" on another Echo device for a quick voice or video chat.

- Say: **"Alexa, Drop-In on [device name]."**

23. Change Alexa's Accent or Language

Switch Alexa's voice to different accents or even another language.

- **How to do it:** Alexa app > **Settings** > **Device Settings** > Choose your Echo Pop > **Language.**

24. Set Sleep Timers for Music

Want to fall asleep to music or relaxing sounds? Set a timer to stop playback automatically.

- Example: **"Alexa, stop playing in 30 minutes."**

25. Ask Alexa for Fun Facts and Jokes

Alexa can entertain you with trivia, jokes, and fun facts.

- Say: **"Alexa, tell me a joke"** or **"Alexa, give me a fun fact."**

26. Use Alexa for Quick Math Calculations

Need to calculate something quickly? Just ask Alexa.

- Example: **"Alexa, what's 25 times 8?"**

27. Find Recipes and Cooking Tips

Alexa can suggest recipes and walk you through cooking instructions.

- Example: **"Alexa, find me a chicken pasta recipe."**

28. Check Sports Scores and Updates

Stay informed about your favorite teams.

- Example: **"Alexa, what's the score of the Lakers game?"**

29. Control Your TV with Alexa

If you have a compatible smart TV or Fire TV, Alexa can control it.

- Example: **"Alexa, play 'Stranger Things' on Netflix."**

30. Enable Skills for More Features

Skills are like apps for Alexa. You can enable thousands of them for games, workouts, news, and more.

- **How to do it:** Say, "Alexa, enable [skill name]," or browse in the **Alexa app** under **Skills & Games.**

31. Get Daily Motivational Quotes

Start your day with inspiration.

- Say: **"Alexa, give me a motivational quote."**

32. Track Your Fitness and Health

Pair Alexa with fitness apps to track workouts and health stats.

- Example: **"Alexa, ask Fitbit how many steps I've taken."**

33. Use Alexa for Calendar and Schedule Management

Sync your Google Calendar or Outlook to manage your schedule.

- Example: **"Alexa, what's on my calendar today?"**

34. Translate Languages Instantly

Alexa can translate phrases for you in real-time.

- Example: **"Alexa, how do you say 'hello' in French?"**

35. Check Package Deliveries

If you shop on Amazon, Alexa can update you on deliveries.

- Say: **"Alexa, where's my package?"**

36. Make Hands-Free Calls and Messages

You can use Alexa to call or message contacts who have Alexa-enabled devices.

- Example: **"Alexa, call Mom."**

37. Ask Alexa to Entertain Kids

Alexa can play kids' songs, tell stories, and help with homework.

- Example: **"Alexa, tell me a bedtime story."**

38. Use Blueprints to Create Custom Skills

With **Alexa Blueprints**, you can create custom skills for your family, like trivia games or personal stories.

- Visit: **blueprints.amazon.com**

39. Enable Hunches for Smart Home Suggestions

Alexa can suggest actions based on your habits.

- Example: Alexa might ask if you want to turn off lights if she notices they are left on.

40. Set Up Voice Profiles for Personalized Responses

Alexa can recognize individual voices and provide personalized results.

- **How to do it:** In the Alexa app, go to **Settings** > **Your Profile & Family** > **Add a Voice ID.**

www.ingramcontent.com/pod-product-compliance
Lightning Source LLC
Chambersburg PA
CBHW071407220526
45469CB00004B/1191